Copyrig

All rights reserved. No part of this book may be reproduced or transmitted in any form or by any means, electronic or mechanical, including photocopying, recording, or by any information storage and retrieval system, without permission in writing from the author.

ISBN: 979-8-218-66295-0

Website: QuantumElevations.com

Cover design by: Monika Maria Meikle, with AI assistance

Interior design by: Monika Maria Meikle

Printed in U.S.A.

Contact information for permissions:
QuantumElevations33@gmail.com

This book is dedicated to my wonderful children

Hadassah, Rebecca, and Isaiah

Thank you for choosing me.

Preface

In a chaotic and demanding world, many seek a deeper sense of purpose, peace, and upliftment. We intuitively sense that there's more to life, a more expansive and fulfilling way of being. It is from this viewpoint and desire for an elevated existence that "Keys to an Elevated Life" was born.

My spiritual journey has led me to an exploration of the connection between the inner world and our outer experiences - the spiritual connection of our thoughts, emotions, and actions. Learning that we create our realities was the spark that started me on this exciting exploration of the interconnectedness of All Things.

Thank you for choosing to embark on this journey with me.

Elevations

Readied for what lies ahead, we are

The journey expansive, directive clear

Earth's Elevation, inhabitants numerous

Humans, plants, and animals

Land and sea do dwell

Compassion, Love and Light

Our mission to fulfill and choose

Choose Elevations

Choose Love, choose Light,

Humanity, and Earth awaits.

-Monika Maria Meikle-

Table of Contents

Dedication... 2

Preface. 4

Elevations 5

Part One: High Vibrational Living 7

Part Two: Awarenes.. 23

Part Three: Nurturing the Physical Being....................... 33

Part Four: Emotions 46

Part Five: Sustaining High Vibrational Living................. 58

Chapter 15: Keys To An Elevated Life............................. 75

Someone to Look Up To.. 78

Acknowledgments. 80

About the Author 81

Part One: High Vibrational Living

Chapter 1: Unlocking Your High Vibrational Potential

Welcome to the journey of creating and maintaining a high vibrational lifestyle. This book, "Keys to an Elevated Life," is designed to guide you on your path to greater happiness, contentment, a fearless existence and a profound realization of the Oneness of humanity and creation. This initial chapter serves as the foundation upon we will build upon towards a deeper understanding of what it means to live life at a high vibration and maintain such.

Simply put, high vibrational living is about cultivating an inner state of connection with positive energies and frequencies. Fine tuning our energies. Just as musical instruments need to be calibrated, so too, our frequencies, emotions, and physical bodies need calibration as well. Lower vibrations are associated with feelings of negativity, stagnation, depression, anxiety, and dis-ease, while higher vibrations are characterized by feelings of love, joy, creativity, enthusiasm, and well-being.

The benefits of embracing a high vibrational lifestyle are manifold. When you consistently operate at a higher frequency, you become a magnet for more positive experiences, opportunities, and relationships into your life. You experience greater resilience in the face of challenges, enhanced mental clarity, increased energy levels, and a deeper sense of purpose. Ultimately, high vibrational living empowers you to live a more fulfilling and meaningful life.

The journey towards an elevated life necessitates a holistic approach, recognizing the intricate interconnectedness of the four fundamental aspects of your being: the spiritual, the mental, the physical, and the emotional. These four pillars are not isolated entities but rather interwoven facets of your overall well-being. Maintaining a consistently high level of vibration requires conscious attention and nurturing of each of these aspects. Neglecting even one area can create imbalances that lower your overall vibration. Therefore, understanding and tending to each facet regularly is key to unlocking your high vibrational potential.

Let us now delve into the significance of nurturing each of these vital aspects:

The Spiritual Aspect: Connecting with Source through Meditation and Vocalized Prayer

Firstly, I would like to point out that, as fractals of Source, we are all resonating at a high vibration, at all times. The spiritual aspect of your being is your connection to something larger than yourself – to All There Is, Was, and Ever, Shall Be. Cultivating this connection is paramount for maintaining a high vibration, as it provides a sense of peace, purpose, and unwavering support.

Meditation: Meditation is a powerful practice that allows you to quiet the chatter of the mind and tap into the stillness, wisdom, love and light of Source. Through consistent meditation, you can reduce stress, enhance self-awareness, cultivate a deeper understanding of self. By focusing your attention and quieting the mental noise, you create space for higher vibrational energies to flow through you. A regular meditation practice serves as a means of fine tuning and aligning your frequencies with the harmonious vibrations of the universe – Source Energy.

Vocalized Prayer: While silent prayer holds its own significance, and has its place, the practice of praying out loud to Source carries a unique and potent energy. Your voice is not merely a tool for communication; it is a powerful instrument capable of emitting sound and vibration. When you articulate your prayers of love of Source and self, gratitude, intentions, hopes, dreams and aspirations aloud, you are actively projecting your energy into the universe. The very act of speaking creates vibrational frequencies that resonates with your desires and connects you more powerfully to Source Energy. Feel the resonance in your chest as you speak your truth and your heartfelt requests. Embrace the power of your voice as a vehicle for divine connection, manifestation, and spiritual elevation.

The Physical Aspect: Nourishing Your Body through Diet and Exercise

Your physical body is the encasement through which you experience life. Maintaining its health and vitality is crucial for supporting a high vibrational state. Just as a finely tuned instrument produces harmonious sounds, a well-nourished and active body is more receptive to higher frequencies, and better able to withstand life's turmoils.

Healthy Diet: The food you consume directly impacts your energy levels and overall well-being. Refraining from refined sugars, a diet rich in whole, unprocessed fruits, vegetables, and minimal animal proteins -fish in particular, provides the necessary nutrients to fuel your body and support optimal functioning. Most fresh, unprocessed foods from the each are alkaline in nature and thus produce an alkaline state within the body. These foods carry higher vibrational energy compared to processed and refined items. By consciously choosing nourishing foods, you are literally feeding your body with higher frequencies, thus, promoting clarity, vitality, and a greater well-being.

Balanced Exercise Routine (Including Cardio): Physical activity is essential for maintaining a healthy body and a vibrant energy field. Maintaining a daily workout routine, including cardio is vital. A balanced exercise routine consisting of general workouts, such as daily yoga, weekly strength training and cardiovascular activity is ideal.

Cardiovascular exercise, in particular, plays a vital role in elevating your vibration. Activities like brisk walking, running, swimming, or dancing increase your heart rate and improve circulation, allowing for a greater flow of energy throughout your body. The goal is to maintain an elevated heart rate for some time, according to your health range and doctor's physicians' recommendations. This increased circulation not only benefits your physical health but also helps to clear stagnant energy and elevate your vibrational frequency. Regular exercise releases endorphins, which have mood-boosting effects, enhancing mood and further contributing to a higher vibrational state.

The Emotional Aspect: Cultivating Meaningful Connections

Your emotional state significantly influences your vibrational frequency. Negative emotions like fear, anger, depression, anxiety, and resentment create low vibrations, while positive emotions such as love, joy, and gratitude elevate your energy field. Nurturing healthy emotional connections with loved ones, as well as acquaintances is paramount for a high vibrational life.

Important Connections with Loved Ones: Human beings are inherently social creatures, and meaningful connections with others are essential for our emotional health. This aspect of our emotional health cannot be overstated. Strong, supportive relationships with loved ones provide a sense of belonging, security, and unconditional love. These positive interactions create a powerful field of high vibrational energy that nourishes your soul and uplifts your spirit. Spending quality time with people you care about, engaging in open and honest communication, and offering and receiving support are vital practices for maintaining emotional balance and fostering a high level of existence. Constantly seek ways to cultivate love and compassion in your relationships further amplifying positive energies. Additionally, for those of us who do not have the benefit of close relationships, daily social gatherings or interactions also serve an important purpose in uplifting the human spirit.

This chapter marks the beginning for understanding the concepts of high vibrational living and the crucial role that the spiritual, physical, emotional, and mental aspects of your being play in achieving and maintaining a high vibration. As we move forward in "Keys to an Elevated Life," we will delve deeper into practical strategies and techniques for consciously cultivating each of these areas, empowering you to unlock your full potential for an elevated and fulfilling life. Remember, unlike a destination, the journey to a high vibrational life is a process of awareness, intention, and consistent effort incorporating all facets of your being.

Chapter 2: What Does It Mean to Vibrate High?

In the previous chapter, we introduced the concept of high vibrational living and its profound impact on our lives. Now, we will delve deeper into the meaning of "vibration" within this context, exploring how our thoughts, emotions, actions, and spiritual practices collectively shapes our overall energetic frequency.

The universe is energy, constantly in motion and vibrating at various frequencies, a cacophony of sound and vibration. Everything within this universe, including we, is composed of this energy and therefore we are all fractals of Source, or similar to and resembling Source Energy. To "vibrate high" signifies that your dominant energetic frequency is aligned with positive, expansive states of being.

The Influence of Thoughts and Emotions:

Our thoughts and emotions are powerful generators of vibration. Positive thoughts, such as love, gratitude, compassion, joy, and optimism, emit high-frequency energy, creating a sense of lightness and well-being within us. Conversely, negative thoughts and emotions like fear, anger, anxiety, depression, and resentment generate lower frequencies, leading to feelings of heaviness, stress, and disconnection from Source.

It is crucial to understand that focusing on positivity does not necessitate the denial or suppression of negative aspects of life. To experience the full spectrum of human existence is to encounter both light and shadow. Rather, in the context of high vibrational living, we learn to **accept and embrace negativity, or contrasting emotions and feelings, as valuable teaching vibrations.** These challenges, when approached with awareness and a desire for growth, can provide profound insights and ultimately contribute to our evolution. We acknowledge these lower frequencies without allowing them to dominate our overall energetic state. Keeping in mind that lower portions of our being are just as much a part of us as our high vibrational being, we shift our thinking to that of acceptance of the contrast within as well as without of our being; and the timely releasing of such, so as to avoid rumination and stagnation which will lead to disease throughout our being. Releasing our contrasting emotions and feelings is vital for maintaining a high level of existence.

The Role of Actions and Spiritual Practices:

Our actions and the practices we engage in also significantly influence our vibration. Acts of kindness, generosity, and service to others radiate high-frequency energy, creating more space for positive energy to flow freely. Conversely, actions rooted in negativity, harm, or inactivity when we have the ability to act in a high vibrational manor, lower our vibrational state. However, keep in mind that **Freedom of Choice is the Greatest Gift We Have – Source**

There is no right or wrong, there is no sin, only high vibrational choices and low vibrational choices. It simply is what it is - choose wisely.

Spiritual practices, such as meditation and vocalized prayer (as discussed in the previous chapter), play a vital role in elevating our vibration by connecting us to higher frequencies of consciousness and Source energy. These practices assist in clearing energetic blockages, promote peace, and align us with Source Oneness.

Vibration Based on Love and Compassion:

At the heart of high vibrational living lies the foundation of love and compassion for oneself and for others. Love is the highest vibrational frequency, encompassing compassion, kindness, understanding, and acceptance. When we operate from a place of love and compassion, the layers of our being resonate with this powerful frequency. In turn, the love frequency attracts more love and positive experiences into our lives. Extending compassion to ourselves, acknowledging our imperfections and struggles with kindness, is equally important in maintaining a high vibration. Self-criticism and judgment create lower frequencies that hinder our spiritual growth.

The Importance of Balance with an Emphasis on Positivity:

The key to sustaining a high vibrational state lies in **balance with an emphasis on positivity.** We acknowledge the presence of both positive and negative energies in our lives, understanding that contrast is essential for growth and appreciation. However, our conscious focus and intention are directed towards cultivating and amplifying positive vibrations. This doesn't mean ignoring challenges, but rather approaching them with a mindset of resilience, learning, and the unwavering belief in our ability to navigate them. Once we have armed ourselves with the spiritual armor necessary to navigate life's tempestuous challenges, we embody the tree that yields and does not break.

By consciously choosing thoughts, emotions, actions, and practices that align with higher frequencies, we actively contribute to the maintenance and elevation of our vibratory being. Much like a muscle that is conditioned, when we consciously choose high vibrational thought and actions, they become second nature over time. This is not about achieving a state of perpetual bliss or denying the realities of life, but rather about cultivating an inner resilience and an energetic alignment with positivity that allows us to navigate life's journey with ease, grace, and fulfillment. Understanding the nature of high vibrational thoughts and actions, and its interplay with every aspect of our being is a crucial step on the path of living an elevated life.

Chapter 3: The Four Pillars of High Vibrational Living

Building upon our understanding of what it means to vibrate high, this chapter introduces the foundational structure for cultivating and sustaining an elevated life: **The Four Pillars of High Vibrational Living.** These pillars represent the core aspects of your being that play an intrinsic role in maintaining a high energetic frequency. They are the **Spiritual, Physical, Emotional, and Mental** dimensions of your magnificent being.

Much like the legs of a table, if one leg is weak or neglected, the entire structure becomes unstable. Similarly, if any one of these aspects of your being is consistently out of balance, your vibration will be compromised, making it more challenging to experience joy, peace, and vibrant health that high vibrational living offers.

High vibrational living necessitates a holistic approach, each dimension is consciously nurtured and tended to. When all four pillars are strong and in harmony, your energetic field resonates at a higher frequency, allowing you to navigate life with greater resilience, clarity, and joy. Keeping in mind that we are Spiritual beings, we are to remember that we all vibrate at a high vibration, spiritually. It is the fluctuation of the other aspects of our being that hinders our spiritual expression. Therefore, the loving maintenance and care of the aspects of our being is critical for increasing and maintaining our vibration.

Moreover, as we cultivate these pillars, it is essential to remember the principle of **moderation and the avoidance of extremes in all things.** We know that it is possible to have too much of a good thing; therefore, moderation is all things is prudent and necessary. For instance, excessive physical exertion without adequate rest and emotional nurturing can lead to burnout. Similarly, intense spiritual practices without grounding in the physical world can create a sense of detachment from our others.

Balance is the key to sustained high vibrational living. This involves finding a harmonious way in which you dedicate your time and energy to each of the four aspects of your being. Create and maintain a meaningful lifestyle without leading to depletion in other areas of your life.

We would be remiss if we did not mention the vital ingredient that needs to be woven into the fabric of our beings: **fun and joy.** Life is meant to be experienced with lightness and enthusiasm. **Joy**

should be sprinkled liberally in everything we do. Make time for activities that bring you genuine pleasure and laughter. **Laugh at yourself and with your others.** Cultivating a playful spirit not only elevates your own vibration but also positively impacts those around you.

Finally, we must take note of **kindness. Be kind to yourself and to your others, always.** Treat yourself with the same understanding and compassion you would offer a dear friend. Recognize that you matter, celebrate your progress, no matter how small, remembering to extend that same kindness and empathy to your others. Being compassionate to oneself as well as others is a powerful vehicle of high vibrational energy, creating positivity and high levels of vibration enhancing your life and the lives of your others.

Notes

Part Two: Awareness

Chapter 4: The Power of Prayer and Intention

The foundational understanding of the four aspects of our being that need to be addressed to achieve high vibrational living has been established, and we now turn our attention to specific practices that actively elevate our energetic frequency. This chapter delves into the power of intention and prayer, particularly within the context of nurturing your being in its entirety and raising your vibration.

The Nature of Prayer:

Prayer is a conscious act of connecting with the Source Energy of our being. It is a way to give praise and adoration, express gratitude, seek guidance, offer supplication, and cultivate a deeper sense of spiritual connection. Prayer manifests in various forms, each holding its own unique power and purpose.

The Vibrational Power of Vocalized Prayer:

The act of praying out loud holds a particularly potent vibrational quality. Your voice is a remarkable instrument, capable of generating sound waves that carry energetic frequencies. When you articulate your prayers, gratitude, and intentions verbally, you are not just expressing words; you are actively emitting a vibrational frequency into the universe.

Embrace the power in the sound and vibrations of our voices. The very act of speaking creates an energetic force that, combined with your intentions, sends signals outward. Feel the resonance in your body as your voice carries your heartfelt expressions. This outward projection of sound amplifies the energy of your prayer, extending its reach and impact on a vibrational level. A dynamic intertwining with Source Energy, a conscious act of co-creation through sound and vibration.

The Role of Silent Prayer:

While vocalized prayer holds significant vibrational power, silent prayer is also possible and has its place. There are times and circumstances where internal reflection and silent communication are more appropriate or necessary. In public spaces and such, where outward expression may not be suitable, the quiet contemplation of silent prayer allows for a personal and intimate connection with Source Energy.

Additionally, when deep-seated issues are felt and need to be expressed internally, silent prayer can provide a safe and introspective space to process emotions, seek inner guidance, and offer heartfelt pleas.

Vocalized Prayer for Vibrational Elevation:

Again, although silent prayer is acceptable at times, the bulk of our prayers should be out loud, where we utilize the powerful magnification of sound and vibration. For the purpose of actively raising your spiritual vibration and extending your intentions into the energetic field, prayer is best when voiced out loud, extending through the universe vibrationally. This practice harnesses the inherent power of sound to amplify your connection and manifest your desires. It is an active participation in the Brilliant Cacophony of the Universe.

Intention Setting:

Closely linked with prayer is the power of intention setting. An intention is a conscious and focused direction of your energy toward a desired outcome. When you set a clear intention, you are essentially planting a seed in the fertile ethers of the universe, signaling your desires and aligning your energy toward their manifestation.

Intention setting works in concert with prayer. While prayer involves vocal dialogue or offering to Source Energy, intention setting is a clear declaration of your desired reality. When you combine the energy of intention with the vibrational power of vocalized prayer, a potent force for positive change in your life is created.

How Prayer and Intention Contribute to a Higher Spiritual Vibration:

Direct Connection to Source: Vocalized prayer facilitates a direct connection to your spiritual Source, bathing you in higher vibrational energies of love, peace, and wisdom.

Amplification of Energy:

Vocalized prayer, in particular, amplifies your energetic output, projecting your intentions and desires into the universe with greater force.

Clarity of Focus:

The act of formulating prayers with setting intentions brings clarity to your desires and aligns your mental and emotional energies with your spiritual aspirations.

Cultivation of Gratitude: Prayer often involves expressing gratitude, which is a powerful, high-vibrational emotion that attracts more positivity into your life.

Release of Lower Vibrations:

Through prayer, you can release feelings of fear, doubt, and negativity, creating space for higher frequencies in your life. Strengthening of Faith and Trust: Consistent intention setting and prayer strengthen your faith and trust in the unfolding of your life's journey.

By consciously engaging in various forms of prayer, with a particular emphasis on the vibrational power of vocalization, and by setting clear and heartfelt high vibrational intentions, you actively cultivate the Spiritual aspect of your being, thus raising your vibrational frequency, paving the way for an Elevated and fulfilling existence.

Chapter 5: Practices for Spiritual Growth:
We have explored the power of prayer and intention in the previous chapter; we now turn our attention to other practices that nurture all aspects of our being, deepening our connection to Source Energy. These practices lead to an elevated vibration,

fostering a sense of peace, clarity, and a sense of participation in the co-creative process.

The Nurturing of Nature:

Spending time in nature is a fundamental practice for spiritual growth and a potent way to connect with the vibrational harmony of Source Energy. The natural world is a seamless extension of the creative process. From the gentle rustling of leaves in the wind to the towering majesty of towering and flowing trees and to the rhythmic crashing of waves. Immersing ourselves in the beauty of the outdoors, allows for the sensitivity of our oneness with nature, thus we become attuned to the naturally higher vibrations of nature.

Grounding in the Early Morning:

Whenever possible, make an intentional effort to connect with the earth early in the morning. This could involve simply standing barefoot on the grass, feeling the cool dew beneath your feet, or sitting quietly amongst the trees as the sun begins to rise. Grounding, or earthing, allows the Earth's natural electromagnetic frequencies to flow with your own, promoting natural stress reduction and a grounded foundation for the rest of your day.

Nature Walks Whenever Possible:

Incorporating nature walks into your routine is another powerful way to foster spiritual connection. Allow yourself to be fully present as you walk, engaging all your senses. Notice the intricate details of the flora and fauna, breathe in the fresh air, and listen to the sounds of nature. These mindful walks create space for reflection, quiet the mental chatter, and allow you to feel the expansive presence of Source Energy in the natural world.

The Power of Mindfulness:

Mindfulness is the intentional focus of your attention on the present moment without judgment. Finetuning the awareness of your thoughts, feelings, and the environment. Incorporating mindfulness into your daily life, even in small instances, deepens spiritual awareness.

You can practice mindfulness while on a walk, performing everyday tasks while eating a meal, or simply breathing. By bringing full attention to the present while taking note of the distractions of the past and worries about the future, thanking them for the teaching gifts they offer and releasing them creates a deeper awareness of the present moment. This allows for deeper introspection and presence of mind and allows you to connect to the subtle energies of Source.

Inner Stillness: Elevation Through Meditation:

Establishing a consistent meditation practice is an invaluable tool for cocreating with Source Energy and elevating your vibration. Meditation provides a dedicated time to quiet the mind, move beyond daily activities, and tune into deeper levels of consciousness with Source.

Through regular meditation, you learn to observe and regulate your thoughts and emotions without attachment or resistance, creating a place of stillness and transformation. This stillness allows you to have access to the wisdom and peaceful presence of Source Energy within you. Whether you prefer guided meditation, silent sitting, or movement-based meditation, consistency is key. Even short, regular sessions can have profound benefits on your spiritual growth and overall vibrational frequency.

When first accessing a meditative practice, guided meditations are an excellent starting point for establishing a spiritual practice "baseline." After a few guided sessions, one should be able to venture out on one's own meditative practice. When establishing a meditative practice, daily events may limit meditation time. At times when time is limited, make time to sit in silence and mindfulness. This is best outdoors, preferably; however, taking five or ten minutes to mindfully sit in stillness creates subtle shifts in your energy field that make a difference in raising your vibration.

By intentionally incorporating these practices into your life – immersing yourself, as much as possible, in nature, establishing the power of introspection and being present through mindfulness, and establishing a consistent meditation practice – you actively strengthen your awareness of the Oneness of all creation, paving the way for an elevated and fulfilling life. These practices are not about escaping the world but rather about deepening your engagement with it from a place of introspection, inner peace, and a more meaningful connection.

Notes

Part 3: Nurturing Your Physical Being & Actions

Chapter 6: The Body as a Temple: Nourishing Your Physical Self

Our physical body serves as the sacred temple that houses our energetic being. Taking conscious care of this vessel through mindful nourishment and movement is paramount for maintaining a high vibrational state. The choices we make regarding what we consume and how we move directly impact our energy levels, overall well-being, and therefore, our ability to resonate at a higher frequency.

Embracing a Health-Conscious Diet:

The food we eat is not just fuel; it is a source of energy and that profoundly influences our physical and energetic systems. A diet rich in whole foods contributes significantly to a higher vibration.

This often translates to a diet consisting mostly of plant-based foods – an abundance of colorful fruits, vegetables, grains, and legumes. These natural sources are packed with vital nutrients, antioxidants - the energy of the earth. Additionally, we must keep in mind that soil depletion necessitates that we include trusted multivitamins into our diets to mitigate against nutrition imbalances that may occur due to the lack of optimal nutrients in the soil

While a vegetarian diet is optimal for peak health and longevity, diverse choices exist. Some may choose to incorporate small amounts of lean poultry, while others may opt for healthy, omega-3-rich fish such as salmon.

Ultimately, the path to nourishing your physical self is a personal one. While research may point towards the benefits of a predominantly plant-based approach, it is crucial to exercise compassion for the diverse choices of our fellow beings. Freedom of choice is a wonderful gift, and we are not to judge one another based on dietary preferences. Our focus remains on conscious and mindful consumption, prioritizing whole, unprocessed foods that nourish our individual temples, and the avoidance of refined sugars.

The Elixir of Life: Mindful Hydration:

A significant portion of our bodies is comprised of water, and as such, water plays a crucial role in countless physiological processes. Proper hydration is vital for maintaining energy levels, facilitating optimal health, including detoxification, and cellular function, all of which contribute to a higher vibration.

It is important to cultivate a mindful approach to hydration. While staying adequately hydrated is essential, we must also be aware of the potential for over-hydration. Our bodies have their own cues, and thirst is one of them. Learning to listen to these signals is key to drinking water when thirsty, ensuring a balanced intake throughout the day – two to three glasses per day is usually sufficient, unless other factors are at play. Pay attention to your body's needs rather than adhering to rigid, one-size-fits-all rules about water consumption.

The Symphony of Motion: The Necessity of Exercise:

Keeping our bodies active and in motion is vital for maintaining physical health, boosting energy levels, and supporting a high vibration. Regular exercise, including **weekly cardio** tailored to your individual health requirements and needs, is a non-negotiable aspect of nurturing your physical vibration.

Cardiovascular exercise, activities that elevate your heart rate and improve circulation, plays a crucial role in this. Whether it's brisk walking, running, swimming, cycling, or dancing, engaging in regular is known to be advantageous and strengthens your cardiovascular system, improves oxygen flow, and has a mood-boosting and stress-reducing effects. This increased action and consequent positive emotional state directly contribute to a higher overall vibration.

Honoring your body as a temple involves conscious choices in nourishment, mindful hydration, and the consistent incorporation of movement. By embracing a predominantly whole-foods diet, listening to your body's thirst cues, and engaging in regular cardio, you actively engaging in the systematic creation of an elevated life. Remember, compassion and non-judgment for the choices of others are integral to this journey

Chapter 7: Movement: I Am Energy, I Am Action

We explored the importance of nourishing our physical selves through conscious dietary choices. Now, we take a deeper into another crucial aspect of physical well-being: movement. This chapter will explore various types of exercise and physical activity, highlighting their ability to release stagnant energy, promote vitality, and raise your vibration.

Our bodies are designed for motion. When we are sedentary, energy can become stagnant, leading to feelings of sluggishness, decreased vitality, and even physical discomfort. Conversely, when we engage in regular physical activity, we stimulate the flow of energy throughout our being, promoting a sense of aliveness and well-being.

The **20 I Am mantras**, as channeled from Source through Elliott Eli Jackson, remind us of a fundamental truth: **"I Am Energy. I Am Action."** This powerful declaration underscores the intrinsic connection between our being and the need for physical movement. Recognizing ourselves as dynamic energetic beings necessitates energetic action as a vital component of our existence.

There are many different forms of exercise and movement that can contribute to this energetic flow:

Yoga: This ancient practice combines physical postures, while emphasizing breathing techniques, and meditation. Yoga is excellent for increasing flexibility, strength, and balance, while also promoting relaxation and stress reduction. Its focus on breathing and mindful movement helps release energetic blockages and cultivate a sense of inner harmony.

Cardio: As mentioned in the previous chapter, cardiovascular exercise, such as running, swimming, cycling, or brisk walking, is essential for elevating your heart rate and improving circulation. This increased blood flow helps to deliver oxygen and nutrients to your cells, boosting energy levels and releasing tension. Cardio is a powerful way to break through stagnant energy and invigorate your entire being.

Weight Training: Building strength through weight training not only supports physical health but also contributes to a sense of empowerment and vitality. Strengthening your muscles helps to improve posture and increase your energy output.

Brisk Nature Walks: Combining the benefits of exercise with the grounding effects of nature, brisk walks in natural settings are a potent way to elevate your vibration. The fresh air, natural scenery, and gentle movement work together to clear the mind, release stress, and promote a sense of connection with the earth's energy.

Dancing: A joyful and expressive form of movement, dancing is a fantastic way to release pent-up emotions, boost your mood, and celebrate the body's natural rhythm. Dancing allows energy to flow freely, promoting a sense of liberation and connection.

Embracing "I Am Action": The Conscious Goal of 10,000 Steps:

In alignment with the profound truth of the **IM mantras – "I Am Energy. I Am Action"** – we are called to make a conscious and deliberate effort to embody this principle through physical movement. As energetic beings, our natural state is one of flow and activity.

Therefore, let us embrace the conscious goal of walking **10,000 steps every day**. This practice is not merely about hitting a numerical target; it is a way to honor our nature as energetic being of action. By intentionally moving our bodies, we stimulate energy flow, support our health, and reinforce the powerful affirmation of our active energetic selves. This daily commitment enables us to embody the "I Am Action" mantra, elevating our vibration.

By embracing movement practices and consciously striving for the daily goal of 10,000 steps, we actively honor our energetic nature as stated in the **I Am Mantras**. This commitment to physical activity is a powerful way to achieve a sense of vitality, release stagnant energy, and elevate your vibration, reinforcing the truth that you are both energy and action.

Chapter 8: Conscious Action: Aligning Your Deeds with Your Intentions

While nourishing our bodies and engaging in physical movement are crucial for a vibrant physical vibration, our journey extends beyond these fundamental aspects. This chapter delves into the profound impact of our daily actions and choices on our overall energetic frequency. It emphasizes the vital importance of living with integrity, where our deeds are a direct reflection of our highest intentions, all while being rooted in love and compassion for ourselves and others.

Every action, no matter how small, sends out a ripple of energetic frequency into the world. Actions born from negativity, dishonesty, or ill-will create low frequencies, contributing to feelings of separation. Conversely, actions anchored in kindness, honesty, and integrity generate higher vibrations, contributing to well-being.

Living With Integrity:

Integrity is the cornerstone of an Elevated Life. It is the state of being whole, where our words, thoughts, and deeds are in alignment with our values. When we act with integrity, we build trust - with ourselves and with others. This creates an energetic match with high vibrational frequencies.

Living with integrity means:

Honesty: Being truthful in our words and actions with ourselves and with those around us. Honoring our commitments and promises encourages trust and creates positive energetic flow. Dishonesty creates low vibrational energy and lowers our vibration.

Accountability: Taking responsibility for our positive and negative actions. Avoiding the blame game, as much as possible, and learning from our mistakes fosters energetic growth.

The Guiding Principles: Love and Compassion:

All of our action must be guided by love and compassion for ourselves and for others. These are the highest vibrational frequencies - the ultimate compass for our choices.

Love for Self: This involves treating ourselves with kindness, understanding, and forgiveness. Self-criticism and judgment hinder our progress. We should recognize our imperfections and struggles with empathy and make choices that nurture our well-being.

Love for Others: Extending kindness, understanding, and empathy to everyone we encounter; acting in ways that alleviate suffering and promote well-being, whenever possible.

When our actions are motivated by love and compassion, they naturally carry a higher vibrational frequency. Even difficult decisions, when made and viewed through the Lense of love and compassion, encourage us to do what is for the highest good.

Oneness:

Recognizing the Oneness of all, without exception, creates an unparalleled unity of existence.

There is No Sin: Realizing that there is not sin – only high or low vibrational choices, emotions, and deeds.

Being Present: I Am Present. Fully engaging in what we are doing, rather than acting on autopilot.

Being Introspective: I Am Introspective. Taking time to review our inner landscape and choices allows for the creation of positive realities for ourselves and the world.

We Are Creators: Accepting the truth that we are all creators of our own realities. Everything that we have done in life, we have chosen to do.

We Are Perfect: Everything we do is done perfectly, with our own signature way of being. We consist of seven perfect systems in synchronization with everything, everywhere.

The above are a few of the 20 I Am Mantras. I highly recommend everyone attain and read the I Am Mantras daily. By doing so, the mantras mesh with your being, elevate your vibration and change your life.

Notes

Part Four: Emotions

Chapter 9: Understanding and Navigating Emotions

Our emotions are a powerful aspect of our being. They serve as signals providing insight regarding our inner state and guide our interactions with the world. Understanding and navigating our emotional being is crucial for elevating our vibration.

Emotions are varied and extensive, ranging from higher vibrational states like joy, love, and gratitude to lower vibrational states such as fear, anger, and depression. While we have a natural propensity towards the positive end of this spectrum, experiencing the full range of emotions is a part of what makes us human. The key lies not in suppressing or denying lower vibrational emotions, but in understanding and processing them in healthy ways, and consciously choosing to cultivate higher vibrational states of being.

The Importance of Releasing Fear:

Fear is a potent lower vibrational emotion that, if left unchecked, can significantly impede our journey towards an elevated life. It often stems from perceived wrongs or threats, both real and manifest in unhealthy thought patterns, such as anxiety, worry, and avoidance. Holding onto fear creates stagnant energy, hindering the flow of positive vibrations and limiting our happiness.

Learning to recognize, accept, be grateful for, and release fear is therefore a critical step in elevating our emotional vibration. This process involves:

Identifying the Source: Gently exploring the root of the fear without judgment. What thoughts or beliefs are fueling this emotion?

Acknowledging the Feeling: Allow yourself to feel the fear without resistance. Trying to suppress it can often intensify it.

Embrace its Message: Asking yourself what this fear might be trying to communicate and decipher what gifts you can learn from its embrace. An important point here is to not hold onto fear for an overly extended period of time.

Gently Release: After expressing gratitude for the gifts that fear has presented you with, which are the ability to feel vulnerability, fragility, and anxiety (gifts). You can now release the spirit of fear with the expressed position of having learned and gleaned what was necessary; therefor fear is no longer needed within your being.

Choosing Mastery: By embracing the I Am Master mantra, we embody inner fortitude and the necessary strength to withstand life's turmoil with grace and mastery.

Practicing Self-Compassion: Being kind and understanding with yourself throughout this process. Releasing deeply ingrained fears can take time and patience; however, be mindful not to take too much time.

Healthy Expression: Finding constructive outlets for emotional energy, such as reading high vibrational books, journaling, engaging in creative expression like art or music, and simply communicating with a friend or loved one.

Physical Movement: Activities like running, dancing, or yoga can help move stagnant energy through and away from the body.

Meditation: Deep slow breathing associated with meditation can be particularly effective in calming the nervous system and releasing emotional tension.

Forgiveness: Realizing that there is no sin; therefore, no need for forgiveness – only acceptance, love, and compassion.

Self-Soothing Practices: Engaging in activities that bring peace and well-being, such as spending time in nature, listening to music, or meditation.

Developing Emotional Intelligence:

Understand and navigate emotions effectively is predicated upon our emotional intelligence, consisting of being aware of your ow emotions, effective emotion regulation, being socially aware, and handling relationships effectively.

By developing our emotional intelligence, we become more skilled at understanding and navigating our emotional landscape and respond to our feelings in ways that support well-being and raise our vibration.

Chapter 10: Positive Emotions:

We explored the importance of navigating our emotions, including the release of lower vibrational states. Now, we focus on the cultivation of positive emotions that elevate our vibration. Gratitude, love, compassion, and peace stand out as potent forces for positive transformation, highlighted in the **I Am mantras** channeled from Source through Elliott Eli Jackson.

I Am Gratitude:

Gratitude is a powerful emotion that shifts our focus to what we already have, instead of the opposite. It is an acknowledgment of the goodness in our lives, both big and small. Practicing gratitude increases happiness, reduces stress, and improves well-being. The **I Am mantra**, **"I Am Gratitude,"** reminds us that when we embody this affirmation, we align ourselves with the high vibrational frequency of appreciation. We foster gratitude by embodying the I Am mantra, gratitude journaling, being grateful and appreciative for all we have and will have, by shifting negative thoughts to things you are grateful for.

to things you are grateful for.

I Am Love:

Love is the highest vibrational emotion, encompassing warmth, connection, acceptance, and the understanding of the Oneness. Love unifies and fosters a sense of belonging. The **IM mantra**, **"I Am Love,"** affirms that love is not something we need to seek externally but is the essence of who we are. By embodying this mantra, we open ourselves to Love's transformative frequency. We foster love by remembering self-love, expressing warmth towards loved ones, seeing the high vibrational aspects of others, and allowing ourselves to be vulnerable.

I Am Compassion:

Compassion is love in action. It is the ability to understand the feelings of others, and desire to alleviate their suffering. It involves the recognition of our shared humanity. The **IM mantra**, **"I Am Compassion,"** highlights that extending understanding and care to others is not just a virtuous act, but a reflection of our true nature. By embodying compassion, we radiate a healing, high vibrational frequency. When we show compassion we practice empathy, show kindness and compassion to others, as well as ourselves.

I Am Peace:

Peace is a state of tranquility, and harmony. It is the absence of conflict and a sense of serenity. Inner peace is essential for maintaining a high vibration, as it allows us to navigate life's challenges with greater resilience. The **IM mantra**, **"I Am Peace,"** reminds us that this state of serenity is not something that is found externally, but a state of being within us. By embodying this mantra, we anchor ourselves in a high vibrational frequency of stillness and calm. We practice a peaceful way of life by daily meditation, spending time in nature, deep breathing exercises, and realizing that control is an illusion,

When we express gratitude, embody love, compassion, and peace, we actively elevate our emotional vibration. These positive states of being create a radiant energetic field that transforms our inner world and positively influences our outer experiences, guiding us towards a joyful elevated life.

Chapter 11: High Vibrational Thoughts: Shaping Your Reality
Our thoughts act like seeds for our emotions and ultimately shape the reality we experience. This chapter speaks to the connection

between our thoughts and our emotional state and introduces practical techniques for identifying and transforming negative thought patterns into positive, high-vibrational ones – **High Vibrational Thinking**.

It's essential to remember that **we are active creators of our reality.** Before incarnating, we chose our parents and designed our life's journey, complete with a **life map** outlining our experiences. Our emotional state plays a significant role in this process, attracting experiences that resonate with our dominant frequencies. Therefore, ensuring high-vibrational emotions is key in shaping a fulfilling reality.

We are the architects of our own realities, and as such, we actively participate in the design of our life journey. We chose our parents and the circumstances of our early existence, fully intending to receive the gifts and growth opportunities they would provide. Furthermore, we each possess an intricate **lifemap**, a blueprint detailing the overarching journey of our life, including key milestones, achievements, and the various experiences intended for our soul's evolution.

While the specifics of this lifemap may not always be consciously accessible, the underlying currents are ever-present. Recognizing our role in shaping our own reality lets us know the critical role of our thoughts. Our thoughts guide our energy and attract experiences that resonate with their vibrational frequency.

Lower vibrational thoughts tend to attract challenging or negative experiences, while high vibrational thoughts, produce positive emotions and experiences of joy, abundance, and connection.

Thoughts and Emotions:

Thoughts and emotions are continuous linked. A negative thought can trigger a negative emotion, which then reinforces the negative thought. Similarly, positive thoughts generate positive emotions, creating an upward spiral of well-being.

Becoming aware of this dynamic is the first step in consciously shaping our reality through high vibrational thinking. By paying attention to our thoughts, we gain insights into our emotional patterns.

Identifying Negative Thought Patterns:

Negative thought patterns sometimes run on autopilot, and learning to identify them is essential for transformation. Common negative thought patterns include catastrophizing, which involves exaggerating potential negative outcomes; all-or-nothing thinking, which leads to seeing things in black and white, with no middle ground; and mental filtering, the tendency to focus only on the negative aspects of a situation and ignore the positive. Other negative patterns include discounting or rejecting positive experiences as unimportant or not genuine; mind reading, or assuming you know what others are thinking, usually in a negative way; and overgeneralization, which means drawing broad negative conclusions. These thought patterns lead to feelings of guilt and frustration. Additionally, negatively labeling yourself or others, and personalization, or taking responsibility for negative events that are not entirely your fault, are also common negative thought patterns.

Techniques for Transforming Negative Thoughts:

Once negative thought patterns are identified, we can begin the process of transforming them into positive, high-vibrational ones. This transformation can be dispelled with the realization that such thoughts are low vibrational entities, and you have the power to instantly send them away by the power of your voice in the name of All There Is Was and Ever Shall be. Once your power to disperse negative entities is activated, gratitude for the dispelling of such, followed by personal affirmations and a grounding meditation if needed. Once we are actively pursuing a high vibrational lifestyle, the power we wield is vast. Finally, we must be in a state of gratitude to maintain heightened sensitivity to surrounding energies, thus being aware when dispelling is necessary, knowing that fear is not necessary when we grasp the power we hold.

By consistently applying these techniques, we can gradually rewire our thought patterns, forming a mindset that aligns with higher vibrational frequencies. As our thoughts become more positive and empowering, our emotions will do the same, and we experience a reality that reflects our mindset. Remembering that, on a soul level, we designed this life, empowers us to take conscious control of our thoughts and step into the elevated reality we have the potential to create.

Notes

Part 5: Integrating and Sustaining High Vibrational Living

Chapter 12: Maintaining Your Four-Fold Being

In summary, we have explored the four essential dimensions of high-vibrational living: nurturing our physical being and elevating our emotional and mental states. We are always at a high vibration spiritually; however, the level of spirituality is predicated upon the health of the other aspects of your four-fold being. Drawing from the core principles and practices detailed throughout this book, these are the strategies for establishing and upholding these practices within our daily lives, shifting them from isolated techniques to integrated and deeply personal ways of being.

The Four-Fold Being

Throughout this book, we've emphasized that high-vibrational living is not achieved through isolated actions but through the harmonious interplay of various facets of our being. The true power of this approach lies in the relationship between these four dimensions. The spiritual aspect of our four-fold being is the most important and relies on the health and well-being of the other aspects of our being.

Physical Well-being: Nourishing Our Temple and Embodying Action As discussed in Chapters 6 and 7, our physical body is our temple, and as such, the way we nourish and move it impacts our vibration. A diet rich in plant-based foods, mindful hydration practices, and consistent exercise, including making an earnest effort to walk up to 10,000 steps daily as emphasized by the "I Am Energy, I Am Action" mantra, are crucial for optimal energy flow. These practices provide an essential foundation for emotional and mental clarity, creating a physical encasement that is capable of holding and expressing higher vibrations.

Emotional Elevation: Love and Compassion Chapters 9 and 10 explored the importance of understanding and navigating our emotions, shifting from lower vibrational states to higher ones. By developing a deeper understanding of our emotions, releasing fear, and cultivating positive states such as gratitude, love, compassion, and peace (as highlighted in the "I Am" mantras), we foster an inner environment that is conducive to higher vibrations. This emotional elevation empowers us to navigate through life with greater resilience, and joy.

High Vibrational Thoughts: Shaping Our Reality with Intention In Chapter 11, we discussed the power of our thoughts in shaping our reality. Our thoughts are powerful creators, actively influencing our perceptions and experiences. By identifying and dispersing negative thought patterns and consciously embracing "High Vibrational Thinking," we align ourselves with the positive outcomes detailed in our life maps. This reinforces positive emotions, creating and self-sustaining cycle of elevation.

Conscious Action: Aligning with Our Highest Self Chapter 8 emphasized the importance of making sure our actions are in alignment with our intentions. When our actions are consistently rooted in integrity, love, and compassion, we vibrate at the highest vibration and become an energetic match for prosperity and abundance, positively influencing the world around us. This high vibrational behavior, like anything else, takes consistent practice until it becomes second nature and runs on auto-pilot – which is our goal when living a high vibrational life.

Practical Strategies for Creating and Maintaining High-Vibrational Living

To effectively maintain your four-fold being in daily life, consider the following strategies:

Morning Ritual: Begin each day with a personalized ritual that starts with love and enthusiastic gratitude. The expression of gratitude within the context of vocalized prayer is the perfect way to start your day. This could also include reciting the "I Am" mantras, along with your personal affirmative statements. Additionally, I recommend implementing a yoga or Qi Gong routine as well. I personally do both and consider them my moving meditations. Lastly, be mindful to make some time to be in nature and in the sun. With the elevated mindset these practices provide, you will be well on your way to a beautiful day.

Mindful Moments: Throughout the day, make it a habit to practice conscious breaks to connect with yourself and meaningfully be aware of your four-fold being. Pay attention to your body's sensations, acknowledge emotions without judgment and breathe deeply while processing them. Observe your thought patterns and, if necessary, practice reframing them in a positive light. Throughout your day, make deliberate choices in your interactions, ensuring they align with integrity, compassion, and love.

Nourishing Meals: Approach each meal as a sacred opportunity to nourish your body and raise your vibration. Practice mindful eating whenever possible, making sure to focus on a meaningful way – a meditation of gratefulness for nourishing food, the ability to feed yourself, and your bodies awesome ability to transform nutrients into fuel for your physical being. Also, express gratitude and appreciation for the company you share your meals with. Meditation in this manor can begin during the loving preparation process of your meals, viewing that process as an act of self-care.

Evening Reflection: Conclude each day with a dedicated period of gentle yoga and introspection. A gentle yoga routine, with specific winding down postures assist in promoting relaxation. The I Am Introspective mantra reminds us to take a non-judgmental look at self, with gratitude and love, reviewing the day's emotional experiences with self-compassion and releasing that which no longer serve your growth. Reflect on the day's positive aspects, identifying ways to further refine your thinking, and thoughtfully evaluate your actions, extending forgiveness for any missteps. Set clear intentions for the following day, remembering your role as the creator of your reality.

Conscious Relationships: Apply high-vibrational living to all your interactions and relationships. This involves expressing love, gratitude, and compassion freely in your relationships, as discussed in Chapter 10. Conscious relationships are those that mirror your sense of self and well-being; seeing eye to eye on spiritual matters is crucial for harmonious relationships when living an elevated lifestyle. Adopting a non-judgmental outlook on all individuals will place you in the position of extending a hand of friendship to all; however, the receptivity of such is up to freedom of choice. And so it is that we choose all and accept that not all are ready to walk the journey with us – perhaps at a later point in time they will be ready. Until then, we and communicate with honesty, kindness, and understanding, focusing on collaborative solutions and aligning our interactions with the principle of Oneness.

Embrace Your Life Map: Throughout this book, we have explored the concept of the life map. During my Life Coach Certification, I received my life map, and it was nothing short of life changing. Suffice it to say that I highly recommend a life map guidance counseling session to assist with life strategy, goals and goal adjustment. Although not religious, the life map is highly spiritual and provides the A-to-Z guidance necessary to live a life of purpose, meaning, and fulfillment.

Consistent Practice: Like any skill, creating and maintaining high-vibrational living necessitates consistent practice and dedication. Have patience with yourself, celebrate every step of your progress, and view challenges as spiritual gifts and opportunities for growth, knowing that you are on your spiritual journey.

Community Support: Seek connection with like-minded individuals who are also deeply committed to living a high-vibrational life. Sharing your experiences openly and supporting one another with compassion builds encouragement, inspiration, and a sense of collective positive energy.

Sustaining a High Vibrational Life

Living a high-vibrational life is not a linear destination but an ongoing process of continuous spiritual growth. By being mindful of every aspect of your four-fold being you form a resilience and vibrancy, empowering you to navigate life's challenges with grace, joy, and alignment with your highest timeline as outlined in your life map.

Chapter 13: Maintaining Your High Vibration

This chapter addresses a crucial aspect of high-vibrational living: how to navigate and transcend the challenges of lower portions of us that can disrupt our journey. We'll explore the concept of energetic matching, understand how our four-fold being influences our vibrational state, and provide strategies for maintaining a high vibration, which minimizes the impact of lower vibrations on our lives.

Becoming An Energetic Match

The universe operates on the principle of energetic matching, often described as "like attracts like." This principle means that the vibrational frequency we emit will attract and cause us to be a vibrational match for high frequencies or low frequencies. When we maintain a high vibration, we naturally draw positive and uplifting experiences into our lives. Conversely, when our vibration is lowered due to our not taking care of an aspect of our four-fold being, we become more susceptible to lower vibrational influences.

The Four-Fold Being and Your Vibration

As we've discussed throughout this book, the spiritual, physical, emotional, and mental make up our four-fold being, and each aspect plays a vital role in determining our vibration:

The Spiritual Being: This is the core essence of our fractal of Source essence. It always vibrates at the highest frequency. However, the degree to which we experience this connection is dependent on the health and alignment of the other three aspects.

The Physical Being: Our physical encasement houses our energy. When we neglect our physical being through poor diet, lack of movement, or inadequate rest, our physical being becomes dense and sluggish, lowering our vibration and lowering the level at which our spiritual being resonates.

The Emotional Being: Our emotions are powerful indicators of our vibrational state. Positive emotions like love, gratitude, and joy raise our vibration, while negative emotions like fear, anger, and sadness lower it. Unresolved emotional issues or suppressed feelings can create energetic blockages that make us vulnerable to lower vibrations.

The Mental Being: Our thoughts create our reality. Positive, empowering thoughts elevate our vibration, while negative, limiting thoughts drag it down. A mind cluttered with worry, doubt, or self-criticism becomes a breeding ground for lower portions of Source.

How Lower Vibrations Affect Us

Lower vibrational frequencies, such as anger, fear, addiction, and despair, can significantly disrupt our lives. When we are energetically matched to these vibrations, we may experience:

Challenging Circumstances: Difficult situations, obstacles, and setbacks may seem to manifest more frequently.

Negative Relationships: We may attract or become entangled with people who drain our energy, exhibit toxic behavior, or reinforce negative patterns.

Emotional Distress: We may struggle with anxiety, depression, mood swings, or other emotional difficulties.

Mental Fog: Our thinking becomes clouded, making it difficult to focus, make decisions, or access our intuition.

Physical Ailments: Prolonged exposure to lower vibrations can weaken our immune system and contribute to physical health problems.

Maintaining a High Vibration: Your Energetic Shield

The key to transcending obstacles and protecting ourselves from lower vibrations lies in maintaining a high vibration. When we operate at this elevated frequency, lower vibrations simply cannot penetrate our aura. It's like playing a game of Pac-Man where maintaining a high vibration is similar to energy pellets shielding us from lower vibrations – it's a superpower.

Here are some powerful strategies for maintaining your high vibration and creating an energetic shield:

Nurture Your Physical Being:

Plant-Based Nutrition: Maintaining a diet of mostly whole, plant-based foods to provide your body with the vital energy it needs.

Regular Movement: Engage in regular physical activity that you enjoy, whether it's yoga, walking, dancing, or any other form of movement that makes you feel alive.

Restorative Sleep: Prioritize quality sleep each night to allow your body and mind to rejuvenate.

Elevate Your Emotional Being:

Emotional Awareness: Stay in touch with your emotions without judgment. Practice healthy emotional processing, such as deep breathing, journaling, or talking to a trusted friend.

Positive Emotions: Pay attention to positive emotions like gratitude, love, compassion, and joy through reciting the I Am mantras daily. Meditation is crucial and should be a daily practice.

Self-Love: I Am Love, I Am Perfect, I Am Radiant, along with all the other I Am mantras, promote self-acceptance and self-compassion. Treat yourself with the same kindness and understanding you would offer a beloved friend.

Empower Your Mental Being:

Positive Self-Talk: Replace negative self-talk with positive affirmations and empowering I Am mantras and be a conscious observer of your thoughts.

High Vibrational Thinking: Consciously choose to focus on positive possibilities, solutions, and empowering perspectives.

Limit Negative Input: Reduce your exposure to negative news, toxic environments, and draining people; however, be mindful to release, not push negativity away, and send lower portions of Source back to their proper place of existence, in the name of All There Was and Ever Shall Be.

Integrity: Live in alignment with your values and principles.

Conscious Choices: Make choices that reflect your commitment to high-vibrational living.

Service to Others: Engage in acts of kindness, compassion, and service to others.

Authenticity: Be true to yourself and express your high vibrational values, gifts, and talents.

Spiritual Connection:

Prayer and Meditation: The foundation of living an elevated life is based on prayer and meditation. Vocalized prayer to Source aligns you with the highest frequencies, allowing for open expression of your heart, while meditation allows for a deeper ability to feel Source frequency. Consistent prayer and meditation practice are vital to raising your vibration and keeping you in what I like to call the purple zone of high vibrations.

Transcending Obstacles with a High Vibration

When you consistently maintain a high vibration, obstacles and challenges still may arise, but your ability to navigate them will be at its best. You will approach difficulties with strength and resilience. Knowing that you have created your reality gives you a new outlook on life – always aware that things are happening for you, not to you.

By consciously choosing to live at a high vibration, you activate your frequency shield, protect yourself from lower vibrations, and align yourself with your highest timeline possible.

Chapter 14: Creating a High Vibrational Environment

This chapter explores how our external environment, including relationships, and media consumption, influences our vibration. Our external environments are a factor in sustaining high-vibrational living.

The Impact of Our Surroundings

Our physical environment plays an important role in our well-being and vibrational state. Cluttered and disorganized surroundings create a sense of chaos that lower our frequency. In contrast, clean, organized, and visually appealing spaces can promote feelings of peace and harmony, thus, raising our vibration. There is some truth to cleanliness being next to Godliness, and our energy levels can attest to it. Keeping a tidy home or work environment can profoundly impact our mental and emotional state. Designating specific areas your home for meditation or yoga, can help to create a sense of peace. A pleasing color pallet and soft lighting can also have a positive effect on our mood and, ultimately, our vibration.

The Influence of Relationships

Our relationships are another aspect of our environment. Positive, supportive relationships act as an uplifting force, while toxic relationships can lower our energy and vibration. Choosing to spend time with like-minded individuals who share our values and support our personal growth is essential for maintaining a high vibration. Engaging in honest communication, practicing empathy, and offering support creates love and trust within our relationships. Healthy boundaries in our relationships are important for protecting our energy from being drained, which means learning to say "no" when necessary, and limiting contact with certain individuals who disturb our peace. Developing a sense of discernment is an invaluable tool in the strategic formation of friendships forming our "inner circle"

The Impact of Media Consumption

With a Master of Science degree in Positive Psychology, I am aware of the tremendous influence of social media and the impact it has on well-being. Although digital platforms can and do serve an uplifting purpose when utilized in a positive way, when creating and sharing values-based stories and information; it must also be said that over-consumption of social media can have a detrimental effect on well-being. Social media consumption should, therefore, be used in uplifting formats and as a tool for the discernment of uplifting Truthful information – avoiding negativity as much as possible, while being aware of its existence and purpose of providing the necessary contrast needed for the reinforcement of peace, love, and gratitude.

Chapter 15: Keys To An Elevated Life

In concluding this exploration, it's vital to emphasize that high-vibrational living is not a destination but a continuous growth process. The key to an elevated existence lies in a steadfast commitment to ensuring our spiritual, physical, emotional, and mental selves function optimally. This holistic approach creates a powerful shield that protects us from lower vibrational influences and allows us to freely navigate life with joyful confidence.

The principles and practices discussed are not temporary fixes but a lifelong processes of our life's journey and path. The understanding of the Oneness of all is also key to an elevated life, ensuring the upliftment of all humans, lifeforms, and elementals.

The Keys to an Elevated Life consist of maintaining a high vibration by nurturing our four-fold being, ensuring optimal levels, fostering a deep connection to Source Energy through personal expressions of love and gratitude.

For those seeking further exploration of my journey and experiences, I invite you to read my book, "Escape from Cultcatraz," which documents my life and journey through restrictive religious cults, and my subsequent spiritual awakening. You can also connect with me and explore more resources on my website, Quantum Elevations Wellness, at QuantumElevations.com.

Thank you for choosing to read this book, which is my offering to the upliftment of humanity.

Notes

<u>Someone to Look Up To</u>

She is smart, she is clever,

She is grounded and centered.

She is someone that lower portions,

Do not attempt to enter.

She does not live in fear

She is always full of cheer.

And, to boot,

She is never drunk on beer.

She is not indecisive,

She does not have many vices,

She is never divisive.

She upright and true blue.

I have not seen her behave cuckoo.

She is not like me and you.

She is, certainly,

Someone to look up to.

    -Source-

Acknowledgments

I would like to express my gratitude to the individuals who have supported me on this journey. First and foremost, to my beautiful mother, Mavis Elfreda Meikle, whose unwavering love and support never wavered, even in the darkest of times.

To my wonderful children Hadassah, Rebecca, and Isaiah, who have taught me invaluable lessons and have given me the opportunity to know unconditional love.

To my master teacher, world renowned channel and author, Elliott Eli Jackson. Your expertise, guidance and Love are invaluable.

About the Author

I am Monka Maria Meikle, Mother, Daughter, Writer, Spiritual Life Coach, and advocate for women, children, and the earth. My work, including my book "Keys to an Elevated Life," focuses on high-vibrational living, healing, and spiritual growth. I am a Certified Hypnotist and an Energy Healer, specializing in a unique modality I have developed called Source Healing Hypnosis, which integrates these powerful techniques. I also hold a Bachelor of Science in Psychology and a Master of Science in Positive Psychology. These academic achievements provide a strong foundation for my understanding of the human mind and the science of human flourishing, which I integrate into my writings and healing work.

I have also written "Escape from Cultcatraz," which is my autobiographical work, chronicling my journey through two restrictive religious cults, and my subsequent spiritual awakening.

You can learn more about my work and connect with me at QuantumElevations.com or via email at QuantumElevations33@gmail.com.

Made in United States
Orlando, FL
18 April 2025